animals
up close

DK

Penguin Random House

Editor Sophie Parkes
Senior Designer Claire Patane
Illustrator Xiao Lin
Pre-production Producer Sophie Chatellier
Senior Producer Amy Knight
Jacket Designer Claire Patane
Jacket Co-ordinator Isobel Walsh
Picture Researcher Sakshi Saluja
Managing Editor Penny Smith
Managing Art Editor Mabel Chan
Creative Director Helen Senior
Publishing Director Sarah Larter

Consultant Derek Harvey

First published in Great Britain in 2019
by Dorling Kindersley Limited
80 Strand, London, WC2R 0RL

Copyright © 2019 Dorling Kindersley Limited
A Penguin Random House Company
10 9 8 7 6 5 4 3 2 1
001–309317–July/2019

A CIP catalogue record for this book
is available from the British Library.
ISBN: 978-0-2413-2739-5

Printed in China

**A WORLD OF IDEAS:
SEE ALL THERE IS TO KNOW**

www.dk.com

CONTENTS

ON THE LAND

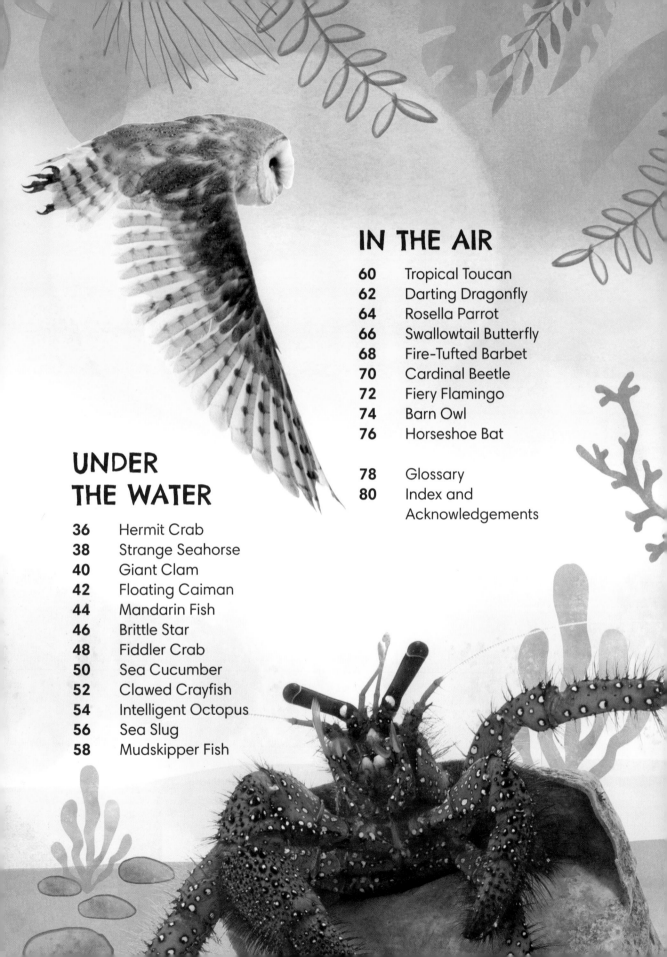

IN THE AIR

UNDER THE WATER

Whiskery Weasel

This woodland creature is one of the smallest furry hunters in the world.

The weasel is no bigger than a guinea pig, but it is a **fierce hunter.** Its prey can be ten times bigger than the weasel itself! A **slim body** and **short legs** allow the weasel to crawl down holes and through cracks in rocks in **search of prey.**

Sensitive whiskers help the weasel to find its way around, especially **at night** and **underground**.

In cold climates, the weasel **sheds** its **brown fur coat** and grows a white coat for winter. This makes it hard to spot in the snow.

Desert Scorpion

Among the most dangerous

creatures in the desert is the scorpion.

It kills prey, such as insects, lizards, and mice, and protects itself with its **stinging tail and powerful pincers**. It can survive in the dry, empty desert for months **without water**, and can live on **a meal of a single insect** for more than a year.

The long, sharp tip on the tail injects **venom** into the scorpion's victim. The effects of this can be **very painful**. Some kinds of desert scorpion can **even kill humans** if their sting is left untreated.

Racer Snake

Shiny green scales hide this snake as it slithers up forest trees.

8

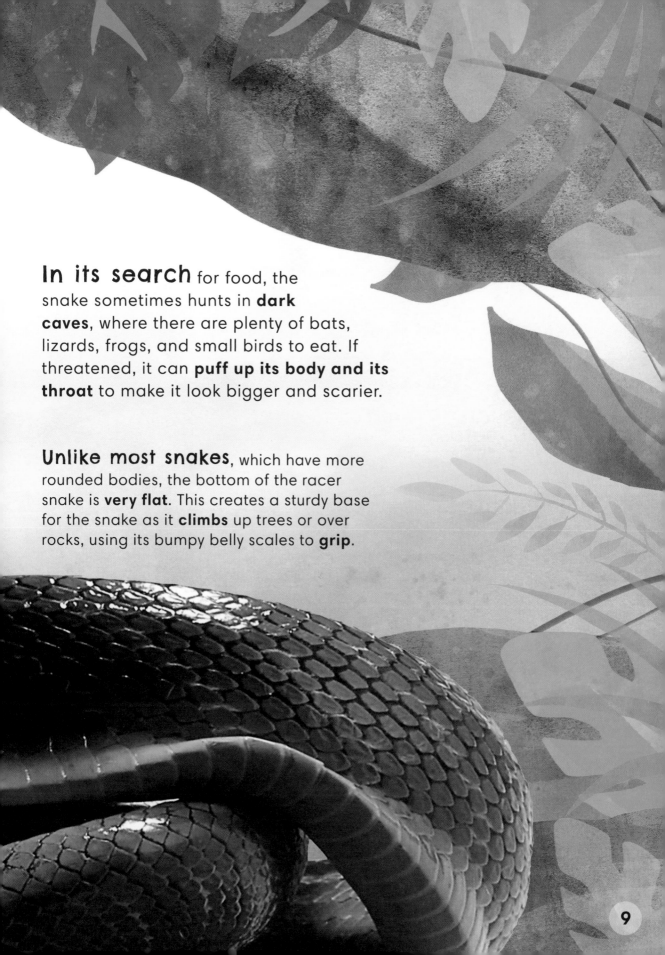

In its search for food, the snake sometimes hunts in **dark caves**, where there are plenty of bats, lizards, frogs, and small birds to eat. If threatened, it can **puff up its body and its throat** to make it look bigger and scarier.

Unlike most snakes, which have more rounded bodies, the bottom of the racer snake is **very flat**. This creates a sturdy base for the snake as it **climbs** up trees or over rocks, using its bumpy belly scales to **grip**.

Harvest Mouse

Fields and meadows with long grass are this tiny mouse's favourite places to live.

It's a speedy climber, and scampers from plant to plant like a monkey in the trees of a forest. It spends summer finding **seeds and fruit** to eat. It eats **as much as it can** to get fat on its body ready for the colder months. In winter, it **shelters from the cold** in a burrow.

Its long tail can coil around almost anything. It acts like an extra hand, **grabbing** onto things and **helping with balance.** The harvest mouse can hang upside down from a stem by **nothing** but its tail!

11

Tough Tortoise

How long can a tortoise live?

Some of them reach 200 years of age.

Scientists can tell how old a tortoise is by counting the **ring patterns** on its shell.

The tortoise moves very slowly using hardly any energy. It is **too slow** to run away from enemies so, in times of danger, it **tucks its head** into its **tough shell** for protection. This tortoise lives in places where conditions are **often quite dry**. In colder mountains, it **hibernates** during the chilliest winter months.

Long claws help the tortoise **pull** itself along the ground.

Disguised Gecko

Meet the Madagascar day gecko –

a master of disguise.

With its bright green scales, this gecko should be easy to spot. In fact, it is difficult to see because it is **hidden** amongst the bright green leaves of its **rainforest** home. An expert climber, it has special **sticky pads** on its toes to help it cling to slippery leaves high in the **treetops.**

Like most geckos, it does not have eyelids so it cannot blink! Instead it has to **lick its eyes** regularly to keep them **clean and moist.**

Tiger Salamander

Here's an odd creature that starts life under the water, then grows up to live on land.

Out of the water, it must stay in **damp places** such as beneath wet leaves or under a log. If **its slimy skin** dries out, the salamander will die.

The female salamander lays eggs in water. When an egg hatches, the young has a long tail, and **breathes through gills**, like a fish. Over time, it grows legs, and its gills are **replaced by lungs** inside its body for breathing air, ready for **life on land**.

Busy Chipmunk

Life in the forest is hard work for this little mammal.

The chipmunk spends most of its time **gathering nuts and seeds** for winter, when it is **too cold** for food to grow. It collects enough to last about six months. It carries the food in **pockets in its cheeks**, which fit as many as seven acorns at a time.

Gathering food is not an easy job when there are **other hungry creatures** about. Usually, about half the chipmunk's store is **stolen** by other animals.

Green Toad

This amphibian can be **found** in many areas of the world.

It can survive in all sorts of conditions – **wet or dry**, **hot or cold**. The green toad **breathes through its skin** as well as its lungs. To keep its skin in good condition, the toad **sheds** it every few days, revealing a **shiny new skin** underneath. It then eats the old skin.

Puss Moth Caterpillar

A tasty treat for birds, this insect protects itself by putting on a scary display.

If an enemy approaches, the caterpillar pulls its head into its body, and puffs up a **bright red ring** around its face. **Two black spots** on the ring look like eyes, so enemies think the caterpillar is a terrifying red-faced creature. It can also **extend red threads** out of its tail and **squirt stinging acid** to scare off enemies completely.

Green and brown patterns on the caterpillar's body help it to **hide** among branches and leaves.

Green Iguana

A leafy branch above a swamp is the iguana's favourite place to sunbathe.

If danger strikes, the iguana jumps into the water below and swims to safety. A **smooth body** makes it a fast mover. **Strong back legs** are good for running up tree trunks and jumping from branch to branch. The iguana **eats plants**, so it doesn't need to hunt for prey, but it does need to **escape** from hungry enemies.

The loose skin hanging below the iguana's chin is called a **dewlap**. The iguana can spread it out like an umbrella to **scare off enemies**.

Partridge Chick

This fluffy partridge chick is up and running just a few hours after it hatches.

The chick's legs look like they bend the **wrong way** at the knee. But what you can see bending is actually the bird's **ankle**.

With its brothers and sisters,
it leaves the nest to join its parents in the
hunt for food. The parents **guard and protect**
it, and **keep it warm**. The chick stays with its
family, which is called a **covey**, until it is
about a year old.

Soft, fluffy feathers, called **down,**
cover the partridge chick. The down traps
a layer of air next to the chick's body to
stop warmth escaping from its skin.

Flying Gecko

High up in the rainforest, this reptile can be spotted gliding from tree to tree.

Flaps of leathery skin on its body and between its toes spread out **like a parachute**, allowing the gecko to glide through the air to **escape danger**.

This gecko is mainly **active at night**, when the temperature is cooler. **Excellent eyesight and hearing** help it find insects to eat in the dark.

A glue-like grip allows the gecko to cling onto branches. The bottom of each of its toes is covered in **tiny hairs**. When the gecko presses its feet against a branch, the hairs **stick in the cracks**, fixing the gecko firmly in place.

Sharp claws grip onto branches, so the marmoset can **jump** through the trees **without falling**. It holds food in its **front paws**, which are a little like human hands.

Mini Marmoset

Tiny and super fast, this monkey is perfectly suited to life in the tropical forest.

Moving very quickly through the tops of the forest trees, there is no room for mistakes. The marmoset **scampers** from tree to tree, stopping to **bite holes** in trunks to get to the tasty gum inside. Its **long, stripy tail** helps it to balance. The marmoset is one of the **smallest monkeys** in the world - it weighs less than a football.

Postman Caterpillar

The menacing spikes on this caterpillar protect it from predators.

When fully grown, the postman caterpillar grows a **tough case** called a pupa. Inside, the caterpillar's body breaks down into a liquid, and then **changes into a butterfly**. This fantastic change is called **metamorphosis**.

Passion flower leaves are the caterpillar's favourite food. It eats about **25,000 times** its own weight in leaves before it turns into a butterfly.

Tree Frog

The leaves of the rainforest disguise this bright green tree frog.

It is hidden from its enemies, but also from the animals it eats. It waits quietly for dinner to come along. It can flick out its **sticky tongue** to catch insects, and uses its **tiny teeth** to grip the largest victims in its mouth.

Huge, bulging eyes can see **all the way** around the frog's head, helping it to spot **moving insects.**

Flat, damp pads on the toes **suck** onto wet leaves and slippery branches.

Hermit Crab

Home for this crab is inside another animal's shell.

Special hairs on its legs help the crab **feel** its way around.

Unlike most crabs, the hermit crab has a **long, soft body**. It must protect it by living in the **empty shell** of a sea snail, where it can **tuck** its body away. The crab can **stretch** its legs out of the shell to pull itself along. It takes its home with it **wherever it goes.**

When the crab grows too big for one shell, **it must move** to a larger one. It **pokes its claws** into empty shells to see if they are large enough.

Strange Seahorse

It is hard to believe that this weird creature is a fish!

The seahorse sucks up as many as **an astonishing 3,500 tiny, shrimp-like animals** in one day. **As it doesn't have a stomach** to hold big meals, this food passes straight through its body very quickly.

It has a head like a horse, a pouch like a kangaroo, and a tail like a monkey. The seahorse can change colour to match its habitat and hide from enemies. It spends most of the day swimming among seaweed and coral reefs. Here, it waits for food, such as shrimps, to pass within reach.

The strong tail grabs onto things in the water, such as coral or seaweed, to stop the seahorse being thrown about by the waves.

Giant Clam

A soft, slimy animal lives inside this huge shell under the sea.

Dots along the shell are actually rows of eyes. They can **sense light**. This helps the clam to spot predators and gives it enough time to **close its shell**.

The clam makes its shell from chemicals in the water. Inside the shell, millions of **tiny green plants**, called algae, grow on the clam's soft body. They **absorb** the clam's **waste** and the clam **feeds** on some of the **algae**. Most of the clam's food comes from algae in this way.

It has no head so the clam **cannot breathe and eat like a human**. Instead, it has two openings on its body. A mouth-like one lets water full of oxygen and food into the body, and a **tube-shaped** one **squirts waste materials** out.

Floating Caiman

This young caiman floats silently in tropical swamps.

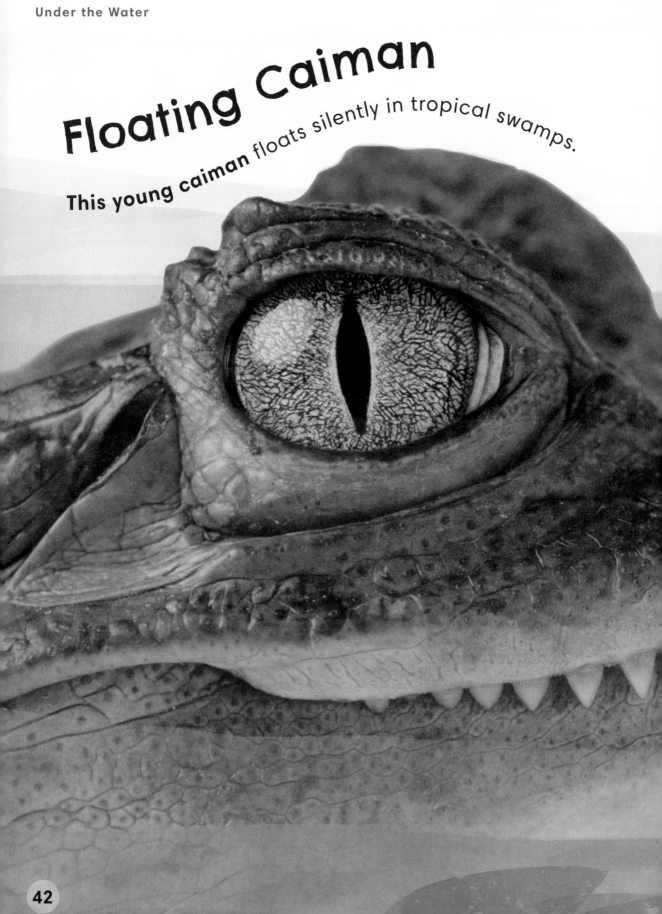

Huge, staring eyes sit high up on the caiman's head, and its **snout turns up** at the end. This means that even when the rest of its body is underwater, the caiman can **see and breathe** in the air. Its ears are covered with **thin skin** to stop water getting inside.

Strong teeth
crunch easily through the shells and bones of the **insects and frogs** that the caiman eats. As the caiman cannot chew, it must **swallow its prey whole**.

Mandarin Fish

The brilliant mandarin fish can be found swimming on coral reefs.

Bright patterns on its skin help to protect the fish from enemies. They warn predators of a **smelly, bad-tasting slime** that the fish's body makes. The mandarin fish can also scare off larger fish by **lifting up the venomous spine** on its back. This trick makes the fish appear **larger** than it really is.

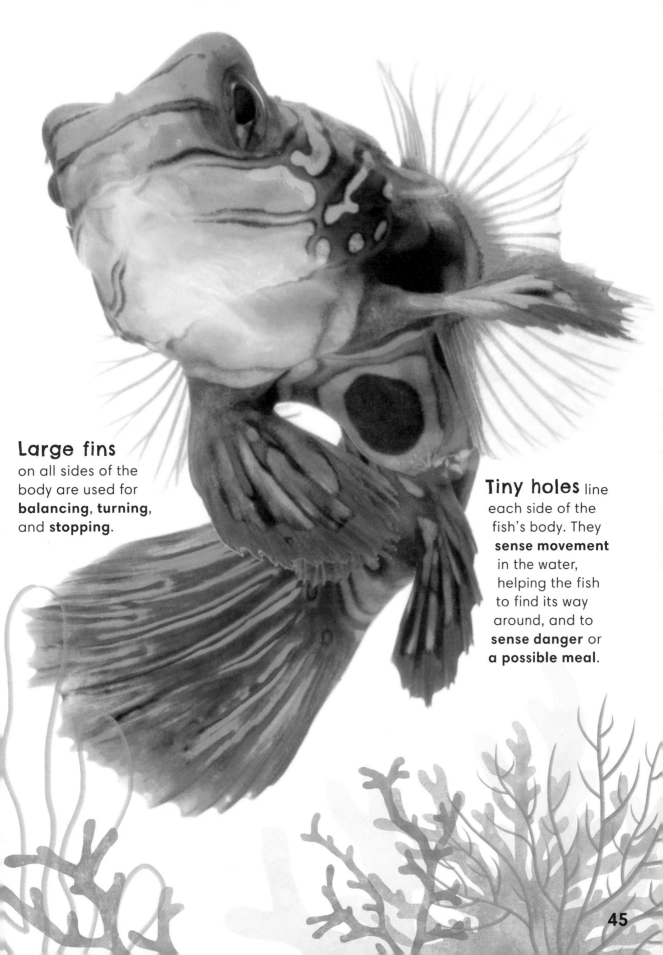

Large fins on all sides of the body are used for **balancing**, **turning**, and **stopping**.

Tiny holes line each side of the fish's body. They **sense movement** in the water, helping the fish to find its way around, and to **sense danger** or **a possible meal**.

Brittle Star

Like its relative the starfish, the brittle star lives under rocks in the sea.

If an arm gets broken off, a **new one grows** in its place, and a **whole new animal** can grow from the lost arm.

This five-armed hunter traps small creatures in the **spikes** on its arms and passes the food into its mouth, which is underneath its body. The spikes are part of the brittle star's **skeleton**. The tips of the arms can sense light and darkness.

Fiddler Crab

When the tide goes out, this crab pops out of its burrow to search for food.

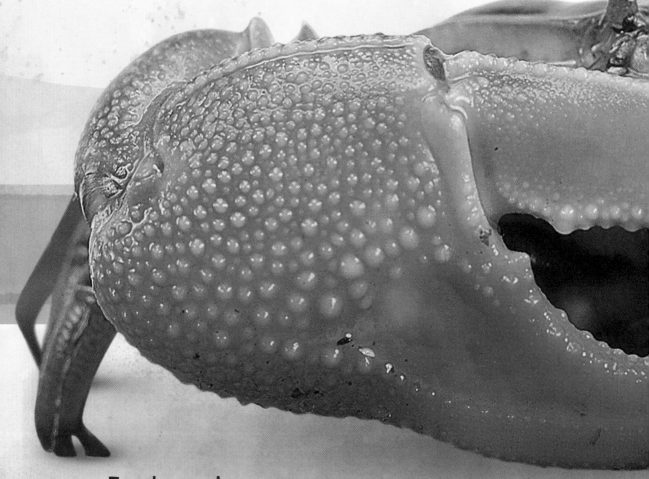

Each crab has its own area on the beach next to the sea or swamp, called a **territory**. The male fiddler crab has **one small claw, and one enormous one**. It uses the giant claw to **signal** to females, and to **wrestle** other crabs that step into its territory.

48

The crab's eyes are on long stalks, so it can **peep** out over the rim of its burrow and **watch for danger**.

Its claws scrape up **balls of mud**, and put them in the crab's mouth. The crab rolls the balls around its mouth, **sucking all the goodness out** of them, before spitting them on the ground. The balls are called "pseudofaeces", a name which means **false poos**.

Sea Cucumber

This strange, squashy sea creature
crawls over coral reefs.

It has no head, just a **mouth** at one end and a **hole to get rid of waste**, called an anus, at the other. When scared, this sea cucumber can **produce poisons** in defence. It can also shoot its insides out of its anus to **save its skin**. A new set of insides grows in a few weeks.

Feathery tentacles

around the sea cucumber's mouth feel for **tiny plants and animals** on the coral reef. It **sucks** this food off the tentacles with its lips.

Bright stripes

down the cucumber's body are actually **many little feet**. **Suckers** on the end of the feet **grip** onto rocks, pushing it along.

Clawed Crayfish

Here's a relative of the lobster that can be found hiding among the weeds in lakes and rivers.

A hard outer coat

protects the crayfish. Large, **grabbing claws** on its front legs are called **pincers**. It uses these for defence, and to dig burrows. It can **flap its tail** to make it shoot backwards through the water at high speed.

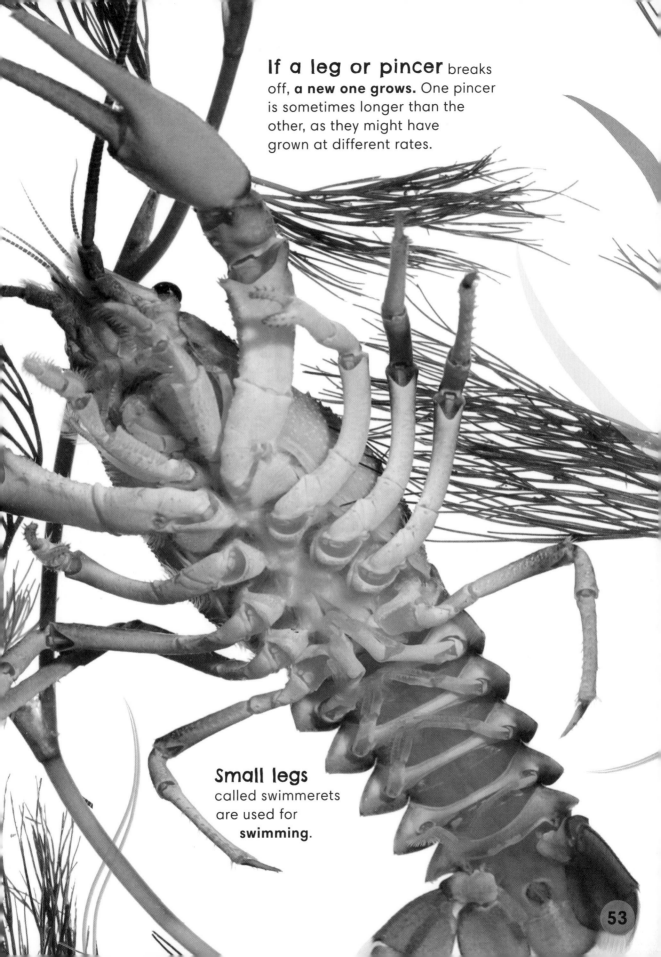

If a leg or pincer breaks off, **a new one grows.** One pincer is sometimes longer than the other, as they might have grown at different rates.

Small legs called swimmerets are used for **swimming**.

Intelligent Octopus

This sea creature is one of the cleverest animals around.

Eight bendy arms with **strong suckers** help the octopus **crawl** along, and curl around victims to trap them. The octopus **bites its prey** with a hard beak, and injects it with poison and special juices to make it easier to eat.

It changes colour to **blend in** with its surroundings, and when its **mood changes**. This octopus turns white when frightened, and red when excited.

The octopus swims by **jet propulsion**. It fills a space in its body with water, and then **squeezes** it back out through a tunnel of skin, **pushing** the octopus through the water.

55

Sea Slug

Although it is related to a snail you might find in your garden, the sea slug doesn't have a shell.

It looks like a leaf, and acts like one too. The green plants the slug eats pass into its **skin**. Here, they keep on working, capturing sunlight and **turning it into energy** by a process all plants use, called **photosynthesis**.

Although it looks tasty, the sea slug produces a **horribly flavoured substance** so that predators don't eat it.

Mudskipper Fish

The mudskipper is very unusual – it is a fish that can walk on land.

Special fins allow it not only to swim, but to **walk, jump, and climb** too. In fact, the mudskipper **moves faster on land**, where it hunts for insects to eat, than in water. Most of its time is spent **out of water**, so it needs to keep its skin **moist**. When it gets too dry, it rolls in puddles, and wipes its face with a wet fin.

Like all fish, the mudskipper breathes by using its **gills** to take oxygen out of the water. **To breathe on land,** it fills **spaces around these gills** with water. These spaces act like oxygen tanks, keeping the fish supplied with oxygen while it is on dry land.

The big beak is **lighter than it looks,** as it is hollow inside. Many **criss-crossed bones** on the outside make it strong.

Tropical Toucan

It's hard not to notice this bird's huge, rainbow beak.

High in the branches of rainforest trees, the toucan uses its beak **to reach berries and seeds** on twigs that are too thin for it to perch on. **Sharp edges** on the beak tear chunks off fruit. The toucan also plays games with other toucans – they use their beaks to **throw fruit** to each other!

61

Darting Dragonfly

The powerful wings of the dragonfly help it zoom around its pond habitat at lightning speed.

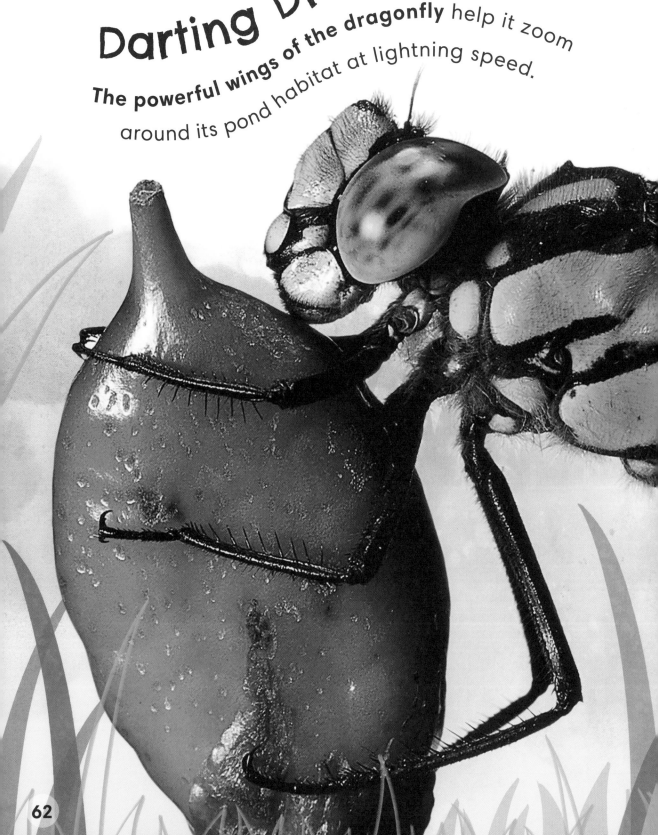

The wings beat about **20 times a second,** pushing the dragonfly along **quickly.** This helps it to chase fast-flying insects. Unlike other insects, the dragonfly **controls each pair of its wings separately,** which helps it to hover, dart backwards, turn sharply, and stop instantly.

The dragonfly can spend many hours in the air **without landing** and often **snatches its meals as it is flying** along.

A long body helps the dragonfly to **balance** as it skims over the water. It is made up of **many sections.**

63

The strong beak is not firmly attached to the parrot's skull. Instead, the top part of the beak **can move separately** from the head, like a swinging door. This makes it easier for the parrot to **grab and eat food**.

Rosella Parrot

This colourful bird can be seen perching in woods and forests.

It is a noisy animal, calling to other rosella parrots to let them know when it has **found something to eat**, and **screeching** to **warn them of danger**. Some clever rosella parrots can be trained to learn tunes or human words.

Swallowtail Butterfly

The bright patterns on this beautiful insect flash in the daylight.

This butterfly can be found **all over the world**. It is named after a bird, the swallow, as the **long, forked shape** of its back wings is the same as a **swallow's tail.**

It eats nectar, the sweet, sugary liquid produced by flowers. **A long tube mouth** sucks up the nectar a bit like a straw sucking up a drink. When the tube is not being used, **it curls up out of the way.**

Bright red spots

on the wings are called **eyespots**. They **confuse** enemies such as birds. Birds peck at the eyespots, thinking they are the butterfly's eyes, which would kill the butterfly. But **only the wings** are damaged.

Its green feathers

help to **camouflage** it in the rainforest treetrops. Like all birds' feathers, they grow out of the skin, and are made out of the same material as **human nails and hair**.

Fire-Tufted Barbet

This rainforest bird is named after the orange-tipped feathers on its beak.

Although it is a bird, the fire-tufted barbet makes a sound very like that of a buzzing bug called a cicada. It loves to feed on figs, and sometimes has to hang upside down from branches to reach them. A **thick, strong beak** helps it to **grab fruit off trees**.

Cardinal Beetle

You could mistake this flying beetle for a tiny red helicopter.

The cardinal beetle

flies around in spring and summer, **feeding** on other insects. The female beetle lays her eggs in the cracks in trees. The young beetles, called **larvae**, eat the larvae of other insects.

Thin wings

transport the beetle through the air. Special muscles in the insect's body move the wings **up and down**.

Red wing

cases protect the wings so they are in good condition for flying. When the beetle is about to fly, **the cases swing up** out of the way of the beating wings.

Fiery Flamingo

Although it starts life as a grey chick, the flamingo soon grows dazzling feathers.

The amazing colour comes from the **pink and orange shrimp** that the flamingo eats. These make it **turn pink** over the first two years of its life. It finds food by paddling in the shallow water of swamps and lakes, using its feet to **stir up food** from the muddy bottom.

Its neck
is one of
the **longest,**
compared to
its body, **of
any bird.**

**A large,
curved beak**
is specially shaped
to **scoop up water**.
Inside are **tiny
fringes**, like the
bristles of a broom.
These **catch** little
plants and animals
in the water for the
flamingo to eat.

Barn Owl

If you hear a blood-curdling screech at night, it could be a barn owl in its nest.

At night, the owl hunts for small animals such as voles, shrews, and mice. It flies silently, low to the ground, **listening** for small creatures moving below. As soon as it hears something, it **swoops down** and **snatches it up** in its large, powerful claws.

The round shape of the owl's face helps to **direct sounds** into the ears on each side of its head. The owl has **excellent hearing**, although you can't see its ears because they are covered by feathers.

Horseshoe Bat

This mammal hunts at night, using a *special* skill to find prey in the dark.

The bat's wings are actually **long fingers with skin stretched between them.** They are very different to the wings of a bird, which are made up of long feathers coming out of the bird's arm bones.

It sends out high-pitched squeaks, which are directed by the **horseshoe-shaped flaps** on its nose. The squeaks **bounce off prey,** such as flying insects, and the bat hears the echo, which tells it where the prey is. This is called **echolocation,** because the **echo** helps the bat **locate** (find) its prey.

Glossary

Algae
Simple plant-like living things, such as seaweed, mostly found in water.

Amphibian
An animal with a backbone that usually spends the first part of its life in water and the rest on land.

Anus
The opening in the body where waste or poo comes out.

Burrow
A hole made in the ground by an animal to shelter or live in.

Camouflage
A colour or shape of an animal that allows it to blend in where it lives.

Down
Soft, fluffy feathers.

Echolocation
A way of finding out where objects are. Animals send out sounds and listen for the echo to work out what is where.

Fish
An animal with a backbone that usually lives in water and breathes with gills.

Gills
Organs for breathing underwater.

Habitat
The place or environment where an animal or plant normally lives or grows.

Hibernate
Spend the winter resting or sleeping.

Hover
Remain in one place in the air.

Insect
An animal with three pairs of legs and a body in three sections.

Jet Propulsion
A way of moving through water or air.

Larvae
The young of some animals such as insects and amphibians.

Mammal
An animal with a backbone that usually has warm blood, fur, and feeds its young with milk.

Metamorphosis
A huge change in shape that takes place for some animals as they grow older.

Nutrients
Substances that are essential for plants and animals for life and growth.

Photosynthesis
The use of sunlight by plants to produce the energy to grow.

Pincers
A claw with two grabbing pieces used for gripping things.

Predator
A hunter that mostly eats other animals.

Prey
An animal eaten by another animal.

Rainforest
A forest in tropical places where a lot of rain falls.

Reptile
An animal with a backbone that lays eggs and is usually covered in scales.

Swamp
A type of habitat that is flooded with water.

Tentacles
Flexible feelers for touching, feeding, or smelling.

Territory
An area where an animal lives or hunts, which it defends.

Tropical
Something from the Tropics, the area of the world that is closest to the Equator (around the middle of the Earth).

Venom
A dangerous liquid produced by some animals to harm prey or defend themselves against attack.

Index

Acknowledgements

DK would like to thank the following people for their assistance in producing this book:
Hélène Hilton for proofreading, Marie Lorimer for indexing, and Barbara Taylor, Theresa Greenaway, and Christiane Gunzi for the original text on which the book is based.

The publisher would like to thank the following for their kind permission to reproduce their photographs:

(Key: a-above; b-below/bottom; c-centre; f-far; l-left; r-right; t-top)

8-9 Dorling Kindersley: Natural History Museum, London / Frank Greenaway (bl). 10 Dorling Kindersley: Liberty's Owl, Raptor and Reptile Centre, Hampshire, UK (b). 18 Alamy Stock Photo: Felix Choo (bl). 28-29 Dorling Kindersley: Jerry Young (r). 42-43 Dorling Kindersley: Jerry Young. 44 123RF.com: Visarute Angkatavanich (c). 45 123RF.com: Visarute Angkatavanich. 46-47 Dorling Kindersley: Natural History Museum, London / Frank Greenaway (b). 52-53 Dorling Kindersley: Natural History Museum, London / Frank Greenaway (r). 52 Dorling Kindersley: Natural History Museum, London / Frank Greenaway (clb, tl). 72-73 Alamy Stock Photo: mohamed abdelrazek. 74-75 Dorling Kindersley: Natural History Museum, London / Frank Greenaway (br). 76 Dorling Kindersley: Natural History Museum / Frank Greenaway (tr). 76-77 Dorling Kindersley: Natural History Museum, London / Frank Greenaway (br)

Cover images: Spine: Dorling Kindersley: Jerry Young (cb)/ (Gecko)

All other images © Dorling Kindersley
For further information see: **www.dkimages.com**